ADVENTURE GAMES

Who doesn't love a good adventure? Tapping into the spirit of adventure is one of the most awesome things that video games can do. Whether undertaking an epic quest battling monsters and exploring a huge world in *The Legend of Zelda*, getting hooked on a great story and memorable characters in *King's Quest*, or searching for items and uncovering collectibles in games like *Grow Up*, there are so many different ways that video game adventures can capture the imagination and so many fun challenges to overcome. In this incredible book, you'll find the adventure game that's perfect for you. We'll introduce you to the best the genre has to offer, taking you to outer space, putting you in the shoes of a superhero, and giving you an expert guide to the classics along the way. We've also got tons of tips and tricks to help you out on your journey, so you've got no excuse to not get out there and start adventuring!

CONTENTS

48

34

28

44

CONTENTS

30

04

26   **16**

EDITOR IN CHIEF
Jon White

EDITOR
Stephen Ashby

SENIOR STAFF WRITER
Paul Walker-Emig

LEAD DESIGNER
Greg Whitaker

DESIGNER
Phil Martin

PRODUCTION
Sanne de Boer, Jasmin Snook

COVER IMAGES
The Legend of Zelda: Breath of the Wild © 2017 Nintendo Co., Inc.
All rights reserved.

Spider-Man © 2016 Marvel Ltd, Sony Computer Entertainment Ltd.
All Rights Reserved

Sea of Thieves © 2017 Microsoft Inc. All rights reserved.

All titles, content, publisher names, trademarks, artwork, and
associated imagery are trademarks and/or copyright material of their
respective owners. All rights reserved.

ISBN 978-1-338-11053-1
10 9 8 7 6 5 4 3 2 1   17 18 19 20 21
Printed in the U.S.A.   40
First printing, February 2017

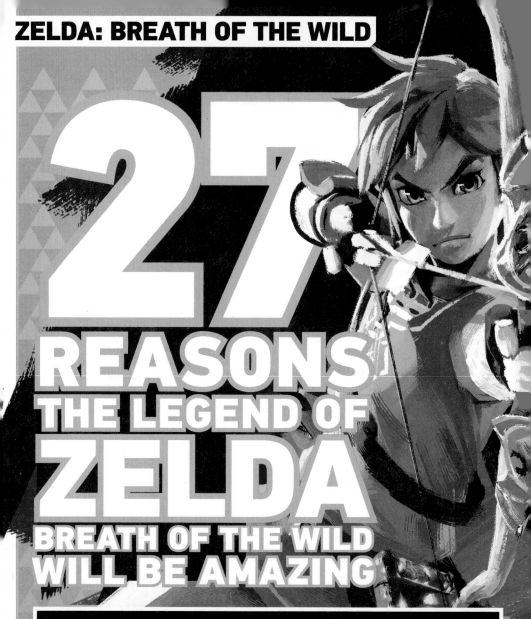

27 REASONS THE LEGEND OF ZELDA BREATH OF THE WILD WILL BE AMAZING

The masters have returned to perfect their craft once more. When Nintendo released *The Legend of Zelda* on the Nintendo Entertainment System back in 1986, it set the bar for adventure games for decades to come. Since then, the dungeons have grown bigger, the weapons more powerful, but the template for adventure remained the same. Until now. Three decades after writing the rules for the adventure genre, Nintendo wants to break them with its most ambitious and daring game to date.

ZELDA IS BACK IN A GAME OF FIRSTS

01 This is the first *Zelda* game on console since 2011's *Skyward Sword*. It's the first (new) *Zelda* game on Wii U. It's also going to be the first *Zelda* game for new console, the Nintendo Switch. Excitement is at fever pitch for *Breath of the Wild* because it's thrilling to see how Nintendo will use the new technology to power the *Zelda* series. Absence makes the heart grow fonder and the consistent quality of the series shows that *Zelda* is always worth the wait, no matter how long that wait may be.

THE COMBAT IS EXCEPTIONAL

03 The baddies are smart, turning what would be boring encounters into unpredictable battles. Enemies run away if they're scared, grab stronger weapons from the floor, and circle you, trying to strike where you can't defend yourself with your shield.

IT WILL LAUNCH THE NEW CONSOLE, THE NINTENDO SWITCH

02 All eyes are on mysterious new console, the Nintendo Switch. *Breath of the Wild* will be one of the first games available on the hybrid console-handheld system. It's exciting to think about what else the new technology could bring to the game.

ZELDA: BREATH OF THE WILD

DAY BECOMES NIGHT... AND THE GAME CHANGES

04 A minute is equivalent to an hour in-game, as the sun sets and darkness takes over. Exploring at night is harder due to limited visibility but some guards and enemies will doze off.

IT'S ALSO A COOKING GAME

05 Not only can you cook food for temporary health benefits, you can also experiment with recipes. Cook up some chillies and you'll stay warm in cold areas!

THE NEW *BREATH OF THE WILD* AMIIBO LOOK INCREDIBLE

06 Three amiibo will be released alongside *Breath of the Wild*: Link as an archer, on horseback, and the intimidating octopus-like Guardian.

YOU NEED TO BE SMART

07 You have to be resourceful to succeed in *Breath of the Wild*. You need to be quiet to avoid being seen by goblins, and you will have to fight against the elements, with freezing cold sapping your health. Beating this adventure will make you celebrate in a way that few other games can.

YOU CAN TRAVEL ANYWHERE

08 If you can see it, you can reach it—as far as it appears. Knowing the beautiful views aren't decoration adds to the sense of adventure.

THE JAW-DROPPING GRAPHICS

09 *Breath of the Wild* is so gorgeous at times, you'll want to stop just to enjoy the scenery. Watching the sunset is mesmerizing, as rays of light pierce through the distant clouds.

THE STORY IS OPTIONAL

10 If you're having more fun exploring the world than following the story, then just ignore the story and explore the world! Nintendo has designed *Breath of the Wild* so you can complete it without ever following the plot.

RUNES OPEN UP INCREDIBLE POWERS

11 Runes in *Breath of the Wild* give Link new powers to play around with. He can summon ice towers to cross water, use magnetism to pluck chests from the bottom of lakes, and even stop time!

MAGNETISM IS FUN

12 Magnetism is one of the first Runes you unlock in *Breath of the Wild*. It's also one of the most useful Runes you'll use, as you can take giant, metallic objects and fling them around as though they weigh nothing.

ZELDA: BREATH OF THE WILD

NINTENDO IS BREAKING CONVENTION AND TRADITION

13 Despite the rich heritage of *Zelda*, Nintendo is brave enough to make changes. *Zelda* games traditionally see Link tackling a series of dungeons, using items picked up along the way to conquer the various puzzles. This time, you complete objectives in the open world, and explore at your leisure. Should you miss the traditional gameplay, shrines still offer a similar mix of puzzles and combat, and there are one hundred to discover!

FIRE GETS EVERYWHERE

14 Hyrule is surprisingly flammable. This can be a great help; you can set fire to boxes or grass to scare enemies. Fire can also be used to solve some puzzles and illuminate areas at night.

IT'S A COLLABORATION

15 It's not just Nintendo creating *Breath of the Wild*. Powerhouse developer Monolith Soft, maker of the brilliant RPG *Xenoblade Chronicles*, has helped create this adventure.

THE MAP IS HUGE

16 *Breath of the Wild* is the largest game in the *Zelda* series … and by quite some margin, too. Its map will be 12 times bigger than *Twilight Princess*. Good luck uncovering all the secrets in this epic outing!

YOU CAN SOLVE PUZZLES YOUR WAY

17 *Breath of the Wild* is full of puzzles that slow your progress but you can solve them in unusual and interesting ways. Need to cross a river? Try creating a breeze for your raft using a giant leaf.

THERE'S AN AMAZING WORLD TO EXPLORE

18 Ruined temples. Distant towers. Green valleys. Goblin villages. It's not just the variety that will floor you, but the detail as well. Poking around the kingdom of Hyrule is fun because you never know what you'll find next.

UPGRADABLE WEAPONS

19 As you travel around the world, you'll grab weapons from enemies that you defeat. The very best weapons will be found in chests, like a giant broadsword, which Link needs two hands to lift. You'll constantly pick up better weapons—which is handy, since weapons can break from overuse!

THE BOSS BATTLES ARE EPIC

20 Each boss in *Breath of the Wild* is unique. Steppe Talus is the stone golem patrolling the Great Plateau. Its rocky hide protects it from swords, so try to bomb its legs. When it topples, quickly strike at the vulnerable spot on its back.

SURF ON YOUR SHIELD

22 It's fun to throw your shield to the ground and leap onto it, riding it down hills like a snowboard. You can even fire arrows while doing this, perfect if you're hunting a particularly fast boar.

YOU CAN HUNT

21 The land of Hyrule feels incredibly alive. You'll see deer grazing in fields and come across boar in the woods. If you want, you can hunt animals for food, or you can take the vegetarian route and pick things like mushrooms to cook instead.

CLEVER REFERENCES FOR FANS

23 *Breath of the Wild* is packed full of clever references and nods for fans to spot. One of the first places you visit is called "Shrine Oman Au." Why is that important? "Oman Au" is an anagram for the surname of producer Eiji Aonuma.

GROWING STRONGER

24 Your health is measured by these hearts. You'll find upgrades that increase the number of hearts, making you stronger.

QUICK SELECT

25 Don't open a menu every time you want an item. Just tap the D-pad to quickly select the right weapon or potion, saving you time.

FLURRY RUSH

26 Jumping out of the way of an attack last minute enables a Flurry Rush. This puts the enemies into slow motion, open for attack.

ITEMS EVERYWHERE

27 Hyrule is huge and you might worry about getting lost. But each quest, chest, and more is flagged on the map to tell you where to go.

NO MAN'S SKY

STATS

Number 1 game on Twitch when released.

216,620 PC owners playing *No Man's Sky* on launch day.

2nd BIGGEST PS4 launch for new series.

5 billion years of playing needed to see every planet.

NO MAN'S SKY

BECOME A SPACE EXPLORER

What is life like beyond our skies? That question is what inspired the creator of *No Man's Sky*, as he looked to the stars and wished he could escape to other worlds. Now you have the tools to find the answer for yourself, as you journey through the universe and discover just how unpredictable space can be. There are worlds with acid rain that corrodes your ship, Amazon-like planets full of curious creatures to discover, and frozen wastelands underneath a bloodred sky to explore. No two planets are the same and the *No Man's Sky* universe has billions of them. You can even name these planets and their strange creatures for other players to find, leaving your very own footprint on space.

TIME LINE

CHECK CONTAINERS
Your first job is to fix your ship. Check containers for valuable resources.

TAKE YOUR TIME
There's no rush, so explore each planet for elements, creatures, fauna, and more.

TOP 5 DISCOVERIES

MONOLITHS

1 These strange, towering sculptures are mysterious and full of intrigue. They also look beautiful against the night sky, especially when lit up by a moon.

RUINS

2 Are they a sign of a previous civilization? Perhaps an alien race that has since abandoned the planet? The more ruins you find, the more questions you will have.

HOSTILE CREATURES

3 Discovering strange alien worlds means you'll sometimes run into the creatures inhabiting them. Some of these creatures are hostile and terrifying, so watch out!

ODD PLANETS

5 Every planet is different and you'll stumble across some planets that are just plain odd, like this planet that's littered with raised, donut-like, stone structures.

DENSE FORESTS

4 Life on alien worlds isn't just limited to creatures. There are fauna and plants to examine, too, and some planets even have dense forests to explore.

REPAIRING SHIP
Your ship repairs automatically with time after combat. Space traders also offer to fix it for you.

EXCITE-O-METER

Discover the universe and make it your own.
+ Infinite exploration
+ Billions of planets
+ A relaxing ride

TIPS & TRICKS
NO MAN'S SKY

8 ESSENTIAL TIPS

MOVE QUICKLY

01 To get around planets faster, there's a clever jet pack trick. Sprint and perform a melee attack, then quickly use your jet pack. The thrust from the melee attack will give your jet pack more momentum.

QUICKER MONEY

02 To quickly earn money, warp around planets to find rare items like venom sacks or pearls. It's better to hunt for rare resources than harvest common ones, which aren't valuable.

FREE EXOSUIT UPGRADES

03 Upgrading your ExoSuit is important, as it lets you increase the number of slots. Check space stations before spending money, as free upgrades can be found orbiting them.

QUICK TRICKS

FIND TRADING POSTS
Scan the solar system while flying in space for a "Trading Post Found" notification.

LOST YOUR QUEST?
Keep warping into new systems until you get a notification of the quest.

HOW TO ALWAYS LAND

04 Aim for your landing spot and as soon as the aiming arrows appear on your HUD, press the landing button. This will ignore trees and rocks, setting you down perfectly and saving you fuel.

SPACE COMBAT

05 Make sure you upgrade your space beam rather than cannons, as the space beam is much more effective. Always keep some Titanium so you can power up your shields mid-combat.

FIND CRASHED SHIPS

06 Instead of buying a new ship, find and fix a crashed ship. Hack a scanner, look for transmissions, activate them, and find a nearby ship.

UPGRADE MULTI-TOOL

07 To open up more slots for your multi-tool, you need to find a new one. You can find multi-tools in space stations or in buildings on planets. You can find them in the machines on the wall that open up as you approach.

REFUELING EASILY

08 You need Thamium9 to refuel your ship and there's a much easier way to do this than searching planets for tiny red plants with the resource. Shooting asteroids will also add Thamium9 to your inventory.

AVOIDING COMBAT
Boost the range of your scanner and height of your jet pack to avoid combat.

LIFE AFTER DEATH
Make sure you return to the spot where you died to recover items from the grave.

SEA OF THIEVES

IT'S A PIRATE'S LIFE FOR ME

It must be exciting being a pirate, right? Exotic lands, swashbuckling tales, and all that buried treasure to find. Or, in the case of *Sea of Thieves*, everyone is belowdecks desperately patching up holes left by cannon fire as water floods the hull. Everyone has a job to do as part of a pirate crew, from firing the cannons, to adjusting the sails, to dropping the anchor. It's the teamwork and camaraderie that make *Sea of Thieves* so much fun, as you form a pirate crew with your friends to go in search of adventure and try to figure out exactly where X marks the spot. And with British developer Rare at the helm, there will be plenty of great humor thrown in as well!

TIPS AND TRICKS

LEAD YOUR SHOTS
Don't shoot cannons at a ship—instead, shoot at where it's going to account for travel.

WATCH YOUR CREW
Always check on your crew's jobs. You'll need to know if your ship is sinking or not.

TOP **5** ADVERSARIES

PIRATES

1 Your main foes in *Sea of Thieves* will be other players. The ocean is a huge place, but when it's swarming with pirate crews, it will feel surprisingly small.

KRAKEN

2 It goes without saying that you have to steer clear of sharks, who won't think twice before taking a curious nibble from your pirate hide. But the mythical Kraken is lurking out there, too ...

THE SEA

3 How can the sea be an adversary? Wait until you enter your first battle. As you take on water and start to sink, you'll realize how deadly the sea can be.

UNDEAD

4 With ghost ships and ghost pirates haunting *Sea of Thieves*'s servers, it's little surprise that skeleton crews show up as well.

YOUR MOTLEY CREW

5 Your biggest adversary could come from within. Teamwork is essential to conquering the seven seas and one slack teammate could jettison your entire adventure.

PLAY WITH FRIENDS

This is the best way to build a crew! Everyone has a job and knows how to work as a team.

EXCITE-O-METER

Arrrrr you ready to set sail?

➕ You get to be a pirate
➕ Battles are a riot
➖ Better with friends

TOP 10
MOBILE ADVENTURES

TALES OF MONKEY ISLAND

The *Monkey Island* series is one of the most well-known in gaming. With treasure hunts, voodoo magic, demon pirates, and the seven seas, it's little wonder they've become so popular. As Guybrush Threepwood, you have to use your wits to solve puzzles and say the right thing to charm your way out of trouble.

MACHINARIUM

There isn't a single word of dialogue in *Machinarium*. Not one. You play as a robot solving a series of brain-bending puzzles to save the city, pushing on in silent determination. Every clue in *Machinarium* is visual, so you have to keep your eyes open and pay attention to the world around you.

BACK TO THE FUTURE

Marty McFly and Doc are back to relive the events of the movie trilogy, and this time you can add your own unique twist to the time-traveling events. You can change famous conversations by switching what the characters say, maybe even changing the outcome altogether. Sometimes it's more fun than sticking to the script!

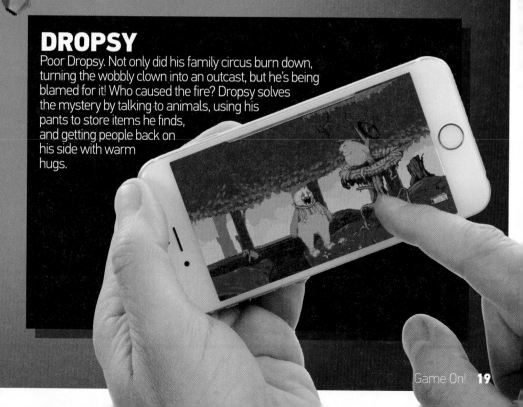

LUMINO CITY

The delicate papercraft world you see in *Lumino City* is real. The developers built a real version of *Lumino City* with paper, cardboard, and string, and that's what you see in the actual game. So tread carefully as you march around the hand-built city solving puzzles—that's someone's hard work you're walking on!

DROPSY

Poor Dropsy. Not only did his family circus burn down, turning the wobbly clown into an outcast, but he's being blamed for it! Who caused the fire? Dropsy solves the mystery by talking to animals, using his pants to store items he finds, and getting people back on his side with warm hugs.

WALLACE AND GROMIT'S GRAND ADVENTURES

The mishaps Wallace and Gromit end up in make for perfect video game material. Across four episodes, the duo deals with giant bees, flooded cellars, golf tournaments, and amusement parks run by dogs. You have to save the day by finding the right use for items you pick up.

JENNY LECLUE

Sharp detective skills are needed in *Jenny LeClue*. You comb crime scenes for clues and examine suspects to see if they're lying. As Jenny tries to clear her mother's name, her adventure takes her through mines, mountains, and even graveyards.

THE DEER GOD

Deer God's hostile world is a constant battle against nature. You're fending off predators like crocodiles and hawks, avoiding deadly drops from clifftops, and dodging hunters. As a reward, you get to explore stunning locations and unlock incredible powers.

LAYTON BROTHERS: MYSTERY ROOM

Investigate mysterious crimes in this police-themed spin-off of the *Professor Layton* series. You need to search for clues, solve puzzles, and put all the pieces together to catch the culprit.

This is the reconstruction device. It faithfully reproduces any crime scene, right down to the minutiae.

Name the Culprit!

"YOU'LL HAVE TO BE AS CRAZY AS THE CREATORS TO MAKE SENSE OF THIS TOPSY-TURVY ADVENTURE!"

STICK IT TO THE MAN

Take a deep breath—this game is the classic tale of a man who can grab thoughts by using a giant arm that sticks out of his brain and slaps those stolen thoughts onto people and places to solve puzzles. Of *course*. You'll have to be every bit as crazy as the creators to make sense of this topsy-turvy adventure.

STATS

18th game in *The Legend of Zelda* series.

12x bigger than *The Legend of Zelda: Twilight Princess.*

2.4 million fans on Facebook.

over **8.5** million YouTube views for official trailer.

THE LEGEND OF ZELDA: BREATH OF THE WILD

A BREATH OF FRESH AIR

The greatest adventure series returns in style. For the first time ever, *Zelda* is moving away from simple A-to-B gameplay and toward a huge open world with *Breath of the Wild*. As Link, you have to find out who destroyed the Kingdom of Hyrule, long lost to the ravages of time since a mysterious disaster 100 years ago. Yet there are so many fun things to do, you might forget your quest altogether. You can throw steak on a fire, watching it sizzle and cook. You can leap on the back of your shield, riding it like a snowboard. You can set fire to grass, watching it spread as enemies flee. Steak, snowboarding, and fire? What more could an adventurer need!

TIME LINE

100 YEARS AGO
A great evil known as Calamity Ganon appears and destroys the Kingdom of Hyrule.

SEALED AWAY
Unable to be defeated, Ganon is eventually sealed away beneath Hyrule Castle.

TOP 5 ZELDA GAMES

OCARINA OF TIME 3D

1 Considered one of the greatest games of all time, the remake of this *Zelda* outing has it all. It has the perfect balance of puzzles, combat, and exploration. Most of all, it feels epic in size and importance, even on a 3DS.

MAJORA'S MASK 3D

2 Moody, gloomy, and mysterious, this time-traveling, 3-D remake is the darkest game in the *Zelda* series. Link needs to replay the same 72 hours over and over to save the land of Termina from a crashing moon.

WIND WAKER HD

3 This glorious outing has a charming cartoon style. *Wind Waker* is bursting with color and light in tone, with more humor than the other games in the series.

THE LEGEND OF ZELDA

5 You can revisit the original adventure thanks to its 3DS re-release. The classic gameplay hasn't aged at all, with tricky dungeons and a wealth of secrets.

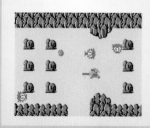

SKYWARD SWORD

4 You can swing the Wii Remote to re-create Link's sword swings in *Skyward Sword*, which makes close battles feel dramatic and often physically exhausting, too.

PRESENT DAY
After a 100-year slumber, Link needs to uncover Hyrule's past and restore it to its former glory.

EXCITE-O-METER

The adventure game returns for its largest outing yet.
+ Fun, tricky puzzles
+ Big, beautiful world
+ A stellar series

TIPS & TRICKS

ZELDA: BREATH OF THE WILD

SLOW DOWN TIME

01 Link can slow down time in *Breath of the Wild*, but don't limit your use of this ability to combat scenarios. You can take the sting out of many traps in dungeons by slowing them down as well.

PICK UP ROCKS

02 Koroks are little wooden people that can be found all over Hyrule. Check dark corners, in bushes, and especially under rocks. They'll be so happy you found them that they will give you a reward.

THE WOLF WITHIN

03 If you have a Wolf Link amiibo, you can scan its code to summon Wolf Link in *Breath of the Wild*. Although you can only do this once a day, Wolf Link will help you in battle by attacking enemies.

QUICK TRICKS

ATTACK FROM A DISTANCE
Use distant arrows or bombs to weaken enemies before engaging with them up close.

SURF YOUR SHIELD
Need to get downhill? Leap on your shield and ride it like a snowboard!

ZELDA: BREATH OF THE WILD

SAIL AWAY, SAIL AWAY

04 If there's water blocking your way, check along the water's banks. Sometimes you'll find a raft, which you can use to cross. You just need a fan to propel the raft. It's faster than swimming!

USING MAGNESIS

05 The Magnesis Rune allows Link to pick up metal objects and move them about freely. You can lift metal blockades away from exits, for example, but also try creating ways to reach secret areas.

HEADS UP

06 The adventure in *Zelda* is as much vertical as it is horizontal. Look for any cliffs you can climb or tall objects that can be moved, so you can head to higher ground. You'll often find secret items there.

EXPLORE THE WORLD

07 You don't need to play through the storyline to complete *Breath of the Wild*, so feel free to explore. Wander off the beaten track and you could find upgrades and items that will make Link more powerful.

COOK YOUR FOOD

08 You gain small benefits such as health and stamina boosts with food. But you gain larger benefits after your food has been cooked, especially if you cook the food in a large batch.

TALK TO EVERYONE
You'll gain clues on what to do by chatting to everyone you encounter.

HIT EVERYTHING
In true *Zelda* tradition, you should hit anything out of place, like cracks in the wall.

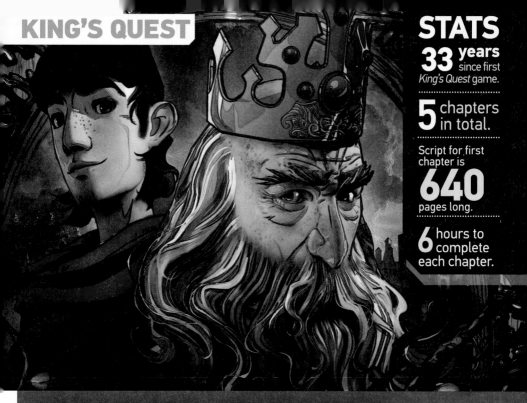

KING'S QUEST
A KNIGHT YOU'LL NEVER FORGET

You're trapped in a cavern with an angry one-eyed dragon. Rickety chains barely hold it back as it snaps its jaws at you. With nowhere to run, do you shoot its chains, letting the dragon free? Trick it into thinking its dinner lies elsewhere? Fire an arrow into its remaining eye? *King's Quest* is full of these dilemmas, giving you a chance to write your own story as a compassionate, wise, or brave knight. You're reliving the adventures of King Graham as he recounts them to his granddaughter. He tells the story according to your actions, so you can sculpt the story however you want. And if you happen to meet an untimely demise? King Graham notes that as he's still alive, that can't be what happened, giving you a chance to try again until you get it right.

TIME LINE

KING'S QUEST
King's Quest started with knight Sir Graham finding treasures to save the Kingdom of Daventry.

KING'S QUEST VII: THE PRINCELESS BRIDE
This game focuses on Queen Valanice rather than Sir Graham.

TOP **5** MOMENTS

STEALING FROM A ONE-EYED DRAGON

1 Your very first quest is stealing a mirror from a sleeping one-eyed dragon. Successfully pulling this off involves hiding in beds, striking dinner bells, and surviving a water raft chase.

JOINING THE TOURNAMENT

2 What's the biggest difficulty in winning the Knight's Tournament? Getting there, as you have to cross a gaping ravine. What makes your job harder are nearby knights interfering with your attempts to cross.

SURVIVING THE GIANT RAT

3 It's not just standard fantasy fare like dragons you need to face. At one point, you'll find a giant rat, and he'd like you for lunch. Maybe you can feed him something else?

BATTLING QUICKSAND

5 When Graham gets stuck in quicksand, he has nearby objects to help. He has an umbrella, buckets, and a skeleton. How does he combine them to escape?

THE PRINCESS AND THE PEA

4 *King's Quest* has a new take on the *Princess and the Pea* tale. The princess is a goblin guarding the pea. You'll need your wits to retrieve the pea.

KING'S QUEST: MASK OF ETERNITY

The most recent *King's Quest* release prior to this one saw the series finally stepping into 3-D and included first-person perspective.

EXCITE-O-METER

An adventure that truly is fit for a king!

✚ Hilariously funny

✚ Write your own story

➖ Tricky puzzles

TOP 8 ADVENTURE STORIES

VALIANT HEARTS: THE GREAT WAR

This touching tale places you in the shoes of men and women from different nations throughout World War I. But even with these different characters, the heart of the story belongs to Emile, a farmer who is drafted into the French army. He becomes the hero of the tale and his final words as *Valiant Hearts* draws to an end are as touching and poignant as video games get.

Judge
Order!
Order in the court I say!

PHOENIX WRIGHT: ACE ATTORNEY

As the bumbling attorney Phoenix Wright, you stumble your way through court cases, using the right combination of evidence and bravado to defend your clients and find the real culprit. As the story develops, eccentric prosecutors try to stop you.

DEPONIA

There's a lot to enjoy in *Deponia*—the smart puzzles, the steampunk setting, the witty dialogue. But most of all, you get to enjoy watching main character Rufus evolve from a difficult child to a hero we can all cheer for.

WHISPERED WORLD

Whispered World takes place in Silentia, the world dreamed up by gloomy clown Sadwick. As the world starts to fall apart, it's up to Sadwick to save it, with the shocking ending making you want to replay the entire adventure again.

DISCWORLD NOIR

Set in Terry Pratchett's famous *Discworld* universe (with the author having written some of the story), you play a private detective who later gets the ability to turn into a werewolf. This helps you solve puzzles using his super sense of smell!

NELLY COOTALOT: THE FOWL FLEET

Take to the seas and meet colorful characters guaranteed to make you laugh. In this charming hand-drawn nautical adventure you search for the Treasure of the Seventh Sea. Just make sure you read all the conversations!

TO THE MOON

Johnny has only one wish—to go to the moon. Sigmund Corp. specializes in implanting artificial memories and grants Johnny his wish by making him believe he's going to visit the celestial body. But as they explore his mind, they find out more about his past and find other memories they wish to alter. *To the Moon* is a bittersweet story that will undoubtedly stay with you long after the credits roll.

NEVER ALONE

Never Alone is a simple game with a big heart. You play as a young girl who sets out with her best friend, an arctic fox, to find out what's causing the eternal blizzard that's threatening their homes.

PAPER MARIO: COLOR SPLASH

TIME TO GET MESSY

Color is fading fast from Prism Island. But who is draining it and why? Toad sends a letter to his old friend Mario asking for help. This plot is really just an excuse for you to get messy with Mario's new Splash Hammer, a giant mallet that splashes color onto anything it touches. *Color Splash* is a role-playing game, and to attack, you have to color in the corresponding cards. When you're not attacking enemies, you can slam your Splash Hammer against the gray environment to fill it with color, revealing hidden items. What really stands out is how gorgeous the game is. This paper world becomes a visual feast as Prism Island lights up with bright colors, so it's clear why Toad is so desperate to save it!

TIME LINE

PAPER MARIO: THE THOUSAND-YEAR DOOR 2004
This sequel added tricks like Mario's ability to fold into a boat or airplane.

SUPER PAPER MARIO 2007
You can now switch between 2-D and 3-D and play as Luigi, Princess Peach, and Bowser.

TOP 5 COOLEST MARIO GAMES

SUPER MARIO MAKER

1 It's the *Mario* game with an infinite number of levels. You create your own masterpieces or download levels created by other players.

SUPER MARIO 3D WORLD

2 Playing as Mario, Luigi, Peach, Toad, or Rosalina, this 3-D platformer is packed with short, tricky levels that are full of secrets to discover.

NEW SUPER MARIO BROS U

3 This colorful 2-D platformer plays like traditional *Mario* games, as you race to reach the flag at the end of the level while avoiding the traps and enemies.

MARIO KART 8

5 Mario and friends race to the finish line. The best part is the items you can use to get ahead, including a Boomerang Flower and Piranha Plant.

MARIO TENNIS: ULTRA SMASH

4 The twist in *Mario*'s take on tennis is the players can use power-ups to balloon in size, allowing them to smash the ball across the court.

PAPER MARIO: STICKER STAR 2012
Mario can use stickers to fight and interact with the world around him, such as a Fan sticker to blow obstacles out of the way.

EXCITE-O-METER

Make a mess without cleaning up afterward.
+ Looks incredible
+ Have fun with color
− Might be too simple

STATS

Announced in
June 2015.

Over
2,500,000+
YouTube views
for E3 trailer.

2 development
teams making
the game.

3 robotic
companions to
help you explore.

RECORE

ONE GIRL AND HER DOG...

As a volunteer for the Far Eden colony, Joule Adams foresaw a bright future. But instead, after hundreds of years in cryosleep, she wakes up to a world where something has gone very wrong. As one of the last remaining humans, Joule needs to find out what happened. Despite its plot, *ReCore* isn't a dark, grungy, post-apocalyptic world. Gun battles light the game up like an explosion in a candy factory, bright colors fizzing and popping as each robot falls. You're not alone, either. You have a robotic dog by your side and you meet other android allies, who lend their unique powers to your battle for survival. It's a companion quest like no other, and with legendary game creator Keiji Inafune at the helm, *ReCore* has plenty of surprises up its tattered, war-torn sleeve.

QUICK TRICKS

ROBOT RESCUE DOG
Your companion is helpful in battle, so let it help out in gun fights if you're taking damage.

PICK THE RIGHT WEAPON
Each weapon has its own distinct use. Experiment with them to test their effectiveness.

TOP 5 GAMES BY RECORE'S CREATOR

MEGA MAN 10

1 *ReCore* creator Keiji Inafune's most famous game is *Mega Man*. He originally designed the character before moving on to making the games themselves, including the extremely tricky *Mega Man 10*.

MIGHTY NO. 9

2 This robot vs. robot platforming game has the spirit of the *Mega Man* series. It's a tricky 2-D platforming game where the key is patience and studying the enemy's patterns.

SOUL SACRIFICE

3 This dark, gothic game for PS Vita is deliberately mysterious. The plot is vague, the setting is strange, and the world is peculiar. You have to learn everything about *Soul Sacrifice* as you play.

Phoenix
Is this the "Mr. Powers" that you saw!?

PHOENIX WRIGHT: ACE ATTORNEY

5 Keiji Inafune was also an executive producer on many Capcom hits, like *Street Fighter 4* and *Phoenix Wright: Ace Attorney*.

LOST PLANET 2

4 If being stuck in a frozen wasteland wasn't bad enough, you have to deal with hostile monsters, too. Few games can match the scale of the battles in *Lost Planet*.

LOOK AROUND

Look high if you're not sure where to go, especially if there are lots of boxes nearby you can climb on.

EXCITE-O-METER

Post-apocalyptic survival has never been this much fun.
+ Gameplay is fast
+ Weapons are fun
− Graphics are so-so

TOP 10
ADVENTURE CLASSICS

DAY OF THE TENTACLE REMASTERED
PC, PS4, Vita

This time-traveling tale sees you trying to stop a giant, mutated, purple tentacle from taking over the world. You have to search every bright, colorful location to find every item you can, from squeaky toys to sweaters, because you never know when they might come in handy.

GRIM FANDANGO REMASTERED
PC, PS4, Vita

It's not every day that you get to play as a travel agent working in the Land of the Dead. Maybe that's why this 1998 classic is every bit as funny and engaging now as it was when it was first released—there's simply nothing else like it. Bursting with creativity, the hilarious gags cover everything from pigeons to the Grim Reaper himself.

SIMON THE SORCERER
PC

When Simon finds a spellbook in his attic, he's transported to another world and finds himself caught up in a battle between two wizards, Calypso and Sordid. Despite the game being over 20 years old, it's still a lot of fun to play. However, some of the puzzles are so difficult, you'll wonder if they require real sorcery.

THE SECRET OF MONKEY ISLAND REMASTERED
PC, PS3, Xbox 360

This could be the greatest adventure game ever made. Playing as the unfortunate Guybrush Threepwood, you have to use your smarts to navigate pirate-filled pubs, abandoned swamps, and cannibal villages. The highlight is a sword fight based entirely on insults, which is every bit as bizarre and amazing as it sounds. You will need to use the right comeback to defeat your silver-tongued foe.

FULL THROTTLE REMASTERED
PC, PS4, Vita

This adventure follows a biker gang as it's framed for a crime it didn't commit. Made by the team behind *The Secret of Monkey Island* and *Day of the Tentacle*, *Full Throttle* has the same mix of funny dialogue and clever puzzles, with the added bonus of motorbike-riding sections.

ANOTHER WORLD: 20TH ANNIVERSARY EDITION

PC, PS4, Xbox One

Following a scientific experiment gone horrifically wrong, Lester wakes up in an alien world. He's immediately chased by a strange, hostile creature. What follows is your battle for survival in a game that's both dramatic and stylish. As an added bonus, *Another World* has easy Achievements and Trophies for you to collect.

TOONSTRUCK

PC

Christopher Lloyd of *Back to the Future* fame stars as cartoon animator Drew Blanc in *Toonstruck*. Blanc gets drawn into the world of his crazy cartoon creations and has to try to save the toon world from an evil force.

ODDWORLD: NEW 'N' TASTY!

PC, PS4, PS3, Vita, Xbox One, Wii U

In this remake of the 1997 *Oddworld: Abe's Oddysee*, you try to escape a meat factory where you're a slave. Solving puzzles is key as you try to creep around the guards.

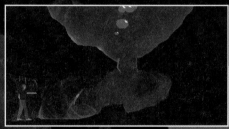

INDIANA JONES AND THE FATE OF ATLANTIS
PC, Wii

It's perfect video game material. Archaeologist Indiana Jones travels the world, looking for hidden treasure and getting into mishaps along the way. *Fate of Atlantis* captures the spirit of the *Indiana Jones* movies, with mysterious locations, fistfights, and complex puzzles galore.

MYST
PC, iOS

Presented with a series of gorgeous still images, you have to click around the pictures to find the clues to solve the puzzles. Despite being so simple, it's the mystery of the setting and the plot that makes *Myst* such a fun game to play, as you have to piece together where you are and how to escape.

150 CRYSTALS
to collect.

4 STAR PLANTS
to grow.

17
Achievements
and Trophies.

24 PLANTS
to find and use.

GROW UP
B.U.D. TAKES TO THE SKIES

Meet B.U.D., an adorable Botanical Utility Droid with some amazing abilities. His job is to journey through space, looking for Star Plants to harvest and return to Earth. However, when his parental ship, called M.O.M., crashes into the moon and breaks into pieces, B.U.D.'s mission becomes a rescue! Take control of the little droid as he jumps, climbs, and explores huge landscapes to collect broken parts, before leaping back down to ground level. Your platforming skills will be tested, but as you explore you'll find and scan plants on the planet that will help you jump high or even launch you into the air. You'll also discover cool new abilities like the jet pack and ball, which help B.U.D. in his quest to save M.O.M.

TIME LINE

GROWING OUT
B.U.D. and M.O.M. explore a new world in *Grow Home* to harvest the seeds of a Star Plant.

GROWING FURTHER
On his second mission, at the start of *Grow Up*, M.O.M. crashes into a moon!

TOP 5 CLIMBING GAMES

GROW HOME

1 B.U.D.'s first adventure was all about growing a Star Plant on an alien world to harvest its seeds. It introduced awesome climbing mechanics, allowing B.U.D. to explore.

THE LEGEND OF ZELDA: BREATH OF THE WILD

2 In Link's latest adventure, he has a skill that he's never had before—he can climb up any surface to explore new areas!

THE CLIMB

4 This VR game is—you guessed it—all about climbing. The main draw, though, aside from scaling cliffs, is the absolutely astonishing visuals, which are sure to blow you away.

SUPER MARIO GALAXY 2

3 Mario's space adventure is as much about gravity as it is about climbing. You'll explore the incredible planets and face tough bosses in Mario's most mind-bending mission ever.

SHADOW OF THE COLOSSUS

5 Taking on huge bosses is the task at hand in this title. To beat them you'll have to climb up their bodies and strike at their weak points. It's a classic.

GROWING BIG

B.U.D. must explore the huge new planet in *Grow Up* to find the pieces of M.O.M. and put her back together.

EXCITE-O-METER

B.U.D.'s biggest adventure yet is great fun!

✛ Massive world to explore
✛ Amazing graphics
✛ Adds new ideas to the series

TIPS & TRICKS
GROW UP

8 ESSENTIAL TIPS

MORE STAR PLANTS

01 Things have changed since *Grow Home*, B.U.D.'s first adventure. Instead of growing one plant into the sky, in this game, there are four to grow and lots of things to collect.

BIRD'S-EYE VIEW

02 Your buddy, P.O.D., flies high above you in the sky and is really useful to give you a bird's-eye view of the level. You can also use P.O.D. to place objective markers to help you get around.

FOLLOW

03 You can go explore wherever you like in *Grow Up*, but you should follow instructions early on. When you get the jet pack and blades, you can start to explore on your own more easily.

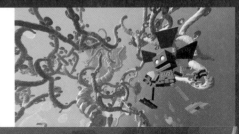

QUICK TRICKS

SUIT UP
New suits, such as a bee suit that attracts bugs, are unlocked by completing challenges.

PLUG IT IN
You need to direct the Star Plant's sprouting branches into the big energy crystals to make it grow.

HOLD TIGHT

04 As soon as you start making your way up to the higher parts of Star Plants, you should hold on tight! It's easy to fall off at any moment, so be cautious with your climbing to avoid any mishaps.

ROLL UP, ROLL UP!

05 Transform into ball mode when you are traveling around the planet to boost, bounce, and roll quickly to your next destination.

GREEN FINGERS

06 New to *Grow Up* is the ability to spawn a copy of any plant you have discovered with the Floradex 3000. Use bouncy mushrooms to reach high places—they're really useful.

CRYSTAL HUNTER

07 Take the time to explore the world and collect as many crystals as you can. They can be used to unlock new abilities that will be a big help to you on your journey.

CRITTER CHALLENGE

08 You can get an easy Achievement or Trophy by picking up one of the critters roaming through the world and finishing a challenge while holding onto it.

PRACTICE CLIMBING

Practice using *Grow Up*'s unique climbing system somewhere safe until you get the hang of it.

BEAM ME UP

Finding teleporters around the map unlocks them and allows you to get around more quickly.

TOP 8 EXPLORATION ADVENTURE GAMES

ABZU

In *ABZU* you take a deep dive into the ocean and swim with schools of fish, ride a turtle's back as a silent passenger, and explore sunken ruins; it's up to you. There is a game to be played and a mystery to be solved. However, it's more fun exploring *ABZU*'s dense and beautiful underwater labyrinths.

BELOW

There's only one place a game called *Below* could be set—underground. The menacing, angular caverns soon give way to spooky tombs. *Below* makes you feel like a tiny explorer among giant ruins.

ORI AND THE BLIND FOREST

Deadly and beautiful, *Ori and the Blind Forest* has retro blood running through its veins. It's inspired by classic 2-D platformers but is modern and fresh.

RIME

In *Rime* you have to figure out what you're doing on the island and how to escape. With no text and no spoken word, you have to rely on your wits and exploration to succeed.

POKÉMON GO

With a map of your local area flagging nearby Pokémon, you have to hunt them down before they disappear. When you have enough Pokémon, you can even battle the leader of the local Pokémon gym and take it over.

JOURNEY

The most aptly·named game ever made, watching *Journey*'s world unfold before your eyes is a joy. You'll slide down sandy dunes, explore towering ruins, squeeze around mountains, and travel through gorgeous scenery.

"WHEN YOU HAVE ENOUGH POKÉMON, YOU CAN EVEN BATTLE THE LEADER OF THE LOCAL POKÉMON GYM AND TAKE IT OVER."

BEYOND EYES

Exploring the world as blind girl Rae means the world around you is a blank canvas. You rely on your senses of hearing and touch to fill in the details.

SONG OF THE DEEP

This cool underwater submarine adventure leans toward combat over puzzle-solving and exploration, which means there are some tough boss battles, too.

LEGO STAR WARS: THE FORCE AWAKENS

CHEWIE, WE'RE HOME

What happens when you combine LEGO and *The Force Awakens*? You'll get an explosion of humor, adventure, and drama, as you experience a hilarious LEGO twist on the movie. You'll also get to see more of the world than the movie's two hours running time could show you, as you explore places like Niima Outpost and Maz Kanata's Castle. Each area is packed with collectibles and secrets tucked away behind puzzles to solve. To match all the action packed into *The Force Awakens*, this LEGO game tilts away from heavy puzzles and toward combat instead. For the first time in a LEGO game, you can take cover, waiting for laser blasts to whistle by before popping up and firing back. Take to the sky in Poe Dameron's X-wing or even fly the Millennium Falcon.

TIME LINE

LEGO STAR WARS: THE VIDEO GAME 2005
The first in the series is based on the *Star Wars* prequel trilogy.

LEGO STAR WARS II: THE ORIGINAL TRILOGY 2006
The original trilogy is revisited, with famous scenes given a dash of humor.

TOP 5 MOMENTS

BATTLE OF TAKODANA

1 The standout moment is the relentless Battle of Takodana. It starts as a shoot-out on the ground but as the battle unfolds, it erupts into a tense dogfight in the sky.

BATTLE OF ENDOR

2 The Battle of Endor is a nice nostalgia trip for fans, while the dense forest makes for a beautiful and unusual battleground.

C-3PO: Were you looking for me?

PLAYING AS BB-8

5 BB-8 stole our hearts in the movie and the little droid will do the same in the game. But being cute doesn't make BB-8 defenseless, as it packs an electrical blast if any guards get close.

OUTSIDE STARKILLER BASE

3 An intriguing blend of stealth, cracking security systems open, and dealing with a huge army of guards.

BEWARE SNOKE

4 You will get a much clearer glimpse of Kylo Ren's mentor, Supreme Leader Snoke, and he really is even more terrifying than in the movie!

LEGO STAR WARS III: THE CLONE WARS 2011
The third in the series was based on the animated series and *Star Wars: The Clone Wars*.

EXCITE-O-METER

Laughter, thrills, and spills with Rey, Finn, and co.

+ Full of adventure
+ Funny twists on big *Star Wars* scenes
+ Lots of characters

TIPS & TRICKS

LEGO STAR WARS: THE FORCE AWAKENS

8 ESSENTIAL TIPS

PRACTICE YOUR MOVES

01 Every character has a unique attack, from Rey's staff slam to Han Solo's pistol blasts. Practice all of these moves before getting into a real fight, so you will know exactly how to defend yourself.

KEEP MOVING

02 When you're taking part in a dogfight, keep swinging left and right. This will make you a harder target to hit, keeping you alive longer. Keep still when aiming your own shots.

THINK BACK TO THE MOVIE

03 Not sure where to go next? It can help to remember the movie and what the characters did there. Remembering scenes can give you a vital clue on where to go or what to do next.

QUICK TRICKS

UNLOCK CHARACTERS
Pause the game, go to Extras, and input the following codes to unlock these characters.

CALUAN EMATT
Entering "26F2CF" will unlock Caluan Ematt, the soldier who recruited Poe Dameron.

STAY BEHIND COVER

04 You can duck for cover when a gun battle breaks out, so make sure you do so. You'll be safe from fire behind cover and you can wait for the perfect opportunity to fire back.

COLLECT PURPLE STUDS

05 You'll find multicolored LEGO studs dotted around each level. They disappear after a few seconds if you don't collect them, so always target purple first—these are the most valuable.

REVISIT LEVELS IN FREE ROAM

06 Replay any level in *The Force Awakens* without character restrictions or story getting in the way.

PLAY WITH A FRIEND

07 *The Force Awakens* lets you play online with a friend, a great way to tackle the game. Work together on puzzles and coordinate attacks.

BUY CHEATS

08 If you're really stuck, you can buy cheats. All you need to unlock new cheats is a Red Brick. These can be bought from D'Qar in the shop or directly from the Character Wheel.

GOSS TOOWERS
Entering "QZTZX9" will unlock Goss Toowers, the Resistance technician of the Shozer.

SNAP WEXLEY
Entering "HTN3RD" will unlock Temmin "Snap" Wexley, pilot of the Blue Squadron.

STATS

Insomniac's **1st** ever licensed game.

34 Spider-Man games to date.

2nd Spider-Man game on PS4.

SPIDER-MAN PS4

DOES WHATEVER A SPIDER CAN

Are you ready for the best *Spider-Man* game ever made? Sony and Marvel handpicked Insomniac Games to create this blockbuster adventure for the Marvel hero, which could even put the *Spider-Man* movies to shame. Insomniac gets to apply its creativity to Spider-Man, and the developer has already promised that it will open up Manhattan for Spider-Man's parkour and web-slinging abilities. Marvel will also work with Insomniac on shaping the story. Unusual for a *Spider-Man* game, it will follow the life of Peter Parker as well as his superhero alter-ego. This really is the *Spider-Man* game that will have everything, and dare we say it, this could be the best superhero game ever.

TIME LINE

RATCHET & CLANK APRIL 2016
The first in Insomniac's series on PlayStation 4, *Ratchet & Clank* releases to strong reviews.

SPIDER-MAN JUNE 2016
At E3, Insomniac announces to the world that it's working on a *Spider-Man* game.

TOP **5** SPIDER-MAN APPEARANCES

SPIDER-MAN UNLIMITED

1 Spider-Man is racing after Sinister Six through Manhattan, dodging the baddies and obstacles in his path as the chase gets faster and faster. This is the fastest *Spider-Man* game you'll ever play!

ULTIMATE MARVEL VS CAPCOM 3

2 Spider-Man finds room for his web-slinging antics, and his unusual movement makes him one of the most unpredictable characters in the game to fight against.

MARVEL HEROES 2016

3 *Marvel Heroes* captures the speed and agility of the web-slinger. Not only can he quickly move around the screen but his in-game Dodge rating means a lot of enemy attacks will miss him.

MARVEL PINBALL

5 Spider-Man's *Marvel Pinball* table features some of the toughest villains he's ever faced. Defeat them all with your pinball skills.

MARVEL ULTIMATE ALLIANCE

4 The main reason to include Spider-Man in your team of four is because he can slow threats down with his web attacks, so the rest of your crew can safely do damage.

SONG OF THE DEEP JULY 2016
Insomniac releases *Song of the Deep*, a game about a girl exploring the depths of the ocean in a sub.

EXCITE-O-METER
With great power comes a great video game!

+ Fantastic developer
+ Graphics look incredible
+ A fun playground

GAMER CHALLENGE

CHECK YOUR GAMING CRED

01 The first enemy you face in *King's Quest* is a one-armed troll. True or false?

02 How many Star Plants does B.U.D. find in *Grow Up*?

03 Which game sees a small plumber exploring space and finding new planets?

04 In what year did *The Last Guardian* begin development?

05 When was the *Virtual Boy* released: 1995, 2001, or 2005?

06 *Paper Mario: Color Splash* is *Splatoon*'s sequel. True or false?

07 What genre of game is *Ori and the Blind Forest*?

08 Who created *ReCore* and *Mega Man*?

09 It will take over 5 billion years to see every planet in *No Man's Sky*. True or false?

10 Which movie is the latest *LEGO Star Wars* game based on?

11 Which game company is making pirate adventure *Sea of Thieves*?

12 In what year was the first *Legend of Zelda* game released?

13 In which time-traveling game can you change history with a conversation?

14 Which spherical droid can you play as in *LEGO Star Wars*?

15 What is Joule's futuristic sidekick in *ReCore*?

16 Who is making the new *Spider-Man* game?

HOW DID YOU SCORE?

0–5 **Gaming noob** – you need to step it up!

6–10 **Casual Gamer** – you could do better!

11–15 **Hardcore Gamer** – you really know your stuff!

16 **Gaming God** – you totally rock!

ANSWERS 01: FALSE 02: FOUR 03: *SUPER MARIO GALAXY 2* 04: 2007 05: A) 1995 06: FALSE 07: A 2-D PLATFORMER 08: KEIJI INAFUNE 09: TRUE 10: *EPISODE VII: THE FORCE AWAKENS* 11: RARE 12: 1986 13: *BACK TO THE FUTURE* 14: BB-8 15: A ROBOTIC DOG 16: INSOMNIAC GAMES

JENTURE

IT ALL BEGAN

As one of the earliest examples of the adventure game genre, this title has had a massive influence on every adventure game that followed it. The game is set in a cave filled with dragons and other mythical creatures. You won't see them, though, because the game doesn't have any graphics! Instead, everything is written in text, explaining to you what you can see and asking you what you want to do. You have to type in commands like "go north," or "look," to interact. As you can probably tell, games have come a long way since!

```
=Introduction=
Somewhere nearby is colossal cave, where others have found fortunes in
treasure and gold, though it is rumoured that some who enter are never
seen again.  Magic is said to work in the cave.  I will be your eyes
and hands.  Direct me with commands of 1 or 2 words.  I should warn
you that I look at only the first four letters of each word, so you'll
have to enter "NORTHEAST" as "NE" to distinguish it from "NORTH".
(Should you get stuck, type "HELP" for some general hints.  For infor-
mation on how to end your adventure, etc., type "INFO".)
- - - - - - - - - - - - - - - - - - - - - - - - - - - - - - - - - -
This program was originally developed by Willie Crowther.  Most of the
features of the current program were added by Don Woods.  The current
version was done by Bob Supnik. This version was implemented on the
IBM-PC (and compatibles) by Kevin Black.

For further information consult your scroll (READ.ME).
- - - - - - - - - - - - - - - - - - - - - - - - - - - - - - - - - -
                        *GOOD LUCK!*

You are standing at the end of a road before a small brick building.
Around you is a forest.  A small stream flows out of the building and
down a gully.  In the distance there is a tall gleaming white tower.
>
```

STATS

20 collectible figurines.

11 playable villains.

10 battle classes such as Knight and Sorcerer.

Over 300 Skylanders toys from previous games can be used.

SKYLANDERS: IMAGINATORS

CREATE YOUR OWN SKYLANDERS

Trigger Happy. Double Trouble. Pop Fizz. These are just three of the many Skylanders you've come to know and love over the years. But can you create something even better? That's what *Skylanders: Imaginators* asks. It gives you the chance to make your very own Skylanders. You decide their powers, abilities, how they look, even their catchphrase. Your creations are teamed up with Sensei Skylanders, who serve as masters to your freshly created Imaginators. They can access Battle Classes, unique weapons, special areas, and more, so it's important to pick the right Sensei as your mentor. Best of all, once you've created your own Imaginator, you store it in a Creation Crystal. You can then take this Crystal to your friend's house and use it to summon your Imaginator, even if they haven't unlocked all the same parts.

TIME LINE

SWAP FORCE 2013
In this game you play as the Swap Force, who have the power to swap body parts and abilities.

TRAP TEAM 2014
The twist with this Skylanders entry is that it introduced Traps, which let you capture villains and play as them.

TOP 5 SENSEI

AMBUSH

1 As Mystical Bamboo Forest's guardian, Ambush has had to keep Kaos's mother at bay, as she wanted its trees for her Royal Courtyard. Armed with a mythic sword, Ambush specializes in fast, damaging strikes.

CHOPSCOTCH

2 Chopscotch uses momentum to swing her giant ax around, creating a tornado of pain for her foes. She can also detach her head, which then becomes a helper in battle.

CRASH BANDICOOT

3 Crash wants to save the Skylanders so he can invite them to a party on Wumpa Island. The famous spin attack is as effective in Skylanders as ever, making short work of enemies.

TRI-TIP

5 There's no subtlety with Tri-Tip. You can charge toward enemies and attack with your head or stay put and swing your Giant Mace instead, which does even more damage.

EMBER

4 Ember commands fire, so she can unleash flaming-hot pyrotechnics to keep enemies at bay. Wielding a dual-blade, Ember's speed and skills mean she's adept at handling any tricky situation.

SUPERCHARGERS 2015
Skylanders + vehicles = *Skylanders: SuperChargers*. Donkey Kong and Bowser were exclusive to Wii U.

EXCITE-O-METER

Build your own Skylanders creation and wreak havoc.

- ✚ You can create Skylanders
- ✚ Lots of creation options
- ✚ Almost all Skylanders toys are compatible

THE LAST GUARDIAN

STATS

In development since

2007.

Originally made for **PS3.**

5,200,000 views for the gameplay trailer.

Only the **third** game made by Team Ico.

THE LAST GUARDIAN

THE MIRACLE GAME

Here's a game that has completely defied the gaming odds. *The Last Guardian* is a touching tale about a small boy and a giant half-bird, half-mammal creature called Trico. Trapped in a strange castle, the two become friends and work together to escape. You play as the boy in *The Last Guardian*, sneaking past guards and climbing around the castle walls, but the creators had a lot of trouble making Trico believable. They wanted this strange creature to react to everything you do like a curious animal would, and PlayStation 3 didn't have enough power to make the game they wanted. But they never gave up on their idea and at last, with the incredible power of the PlayStation 4 behind it, this creative game has finally been turned from a dream into reality.

TIME LINE

THE LAST GUARDIAN ANNOUNCED 2007
Team Ico announces *The Last Guardian.*

THE LAST GUARDIAN DISAPPEARS 2011
Despite the excitement, the creators of the game go silent.

TOP 5 WAYS TO USE TRICO

THROWING BARRELS

1 Sometimes you need to climb Trico's back to reach higher platforms. Throw a barrel at where you want him to stand and he'll wander over to investigate the sound.

DISTRACTING GUARDS

2 As a massive creature, Trico is easily spotted by guards, who do their best to recapture their former prisoner. This allows you to sneak past those distracted guards.

FINDING THE WAY AHEAD

3 If you aren't sure where to go next, watch Trico. When the creature is left alone, it will sniff around the castle walls and sometimes it will spot a hidden area.

USING LIGHTNING

4 If Trico gets into trouble, it can defend itself by firing lightning from its tail. You just need to keep your distance when this happens, so you don't get accidentally hit.

COMPANIONSHIP

5 The castle you're trapped in is a strange, scary place. But as your time with Trico grows, it will learn to trust you and eventually, it will even look after you.

EXCITE-O-METER

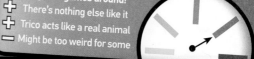

THE LAST GUARDIAN REEMERGES 2015
The Last Guardian is back, prepped for release on PlayStation 4.

One of the most interesting and exciting PS4 games around!

➕ There's nothing else like it
➕ Trico acts like a real animal
➖ Might be too weird for some

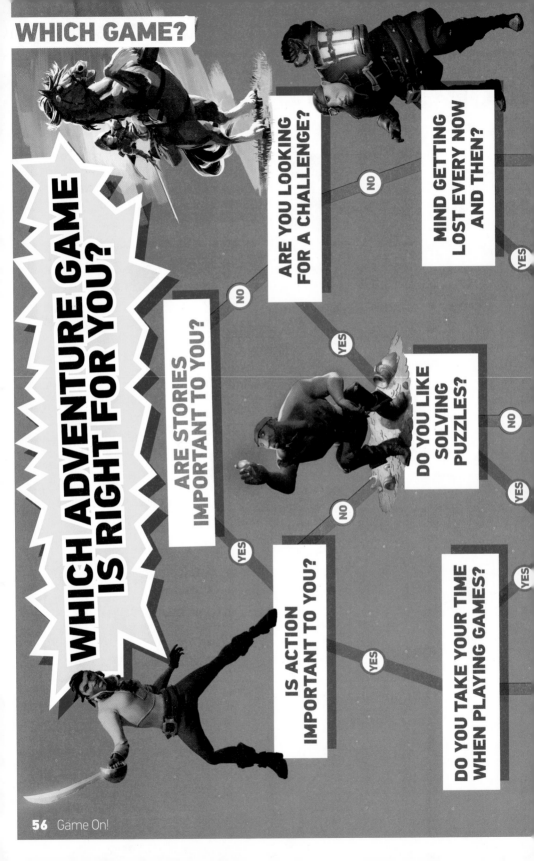

WHICH ADVENTURE GAME IS RIGHT FOR YOU?

ARE STORIES IMPORTANT TO YOU?

NO

YES

ARE YOU LOOKING FOR A CHALLENGE?

NO

YES

MIND GETTING LOST EVERY NOW AND THEN?

YES

DO YOU LIKE SOLVING PUZZLES?

NO

YES

IS ACTION IMPORTANT TO YOU?

NO

YES

DO YOU TAKE YOUR TIME WHEN PLAYING GAMES?

YES

DO YOU PREFER THE SEA OVER SPACE?

NO

YES

NO

DO YOU PREFER THE COMPANY OF ANIMALS OVER HUMANS?

NO

YES

ARE YOU LOOKING FOR LOTS OF ACTION?

NO

YES

NO

NO MAN'S SKY
Explore the farthest reaches of the universe and discover things no man has seen before.

SEA OF THIEVES
Together with your pirate friends, sail the seven seas. Look for treasure and battle rival pirate crews.

ZELDA: BREATH OF THE WILD
Link wakes up after 100 years of sleep in his quest to defeat the evil Calamity Ganon.

ABZU
Dive into the ocean and get lost among sunken ships, lost cities, and the curious sea creatures that swim with you.

KING'S QUEST
In this fun game you get to write your own story of legend, from saving maidens to defeating one-eyed dragons.

LEGO STAR WARS: THE FORCE AWAKENS
Relive the best *The Force Awakens* moments, and explore iconic locations.

MOST AWESOME ADVENTURE ACHIEVEMENTS & TROPHIES!

EARN THE BIGGEST PRIZES ON YOUR ADVENTURES

Adventure games are fun because they let us explore worlds we could only dream of. We can slide down sandy mountains with crumbling ruins blocking out the scorching sun or explore the darkest depths of the ocean. But getting to satisfy your curiosity and thirst for new lands isn't your only reward for embarking on adventures. Each game is also packed with achievements, which are rewarded for completing certain challenges while playing. Some of them are easy, some of them are tricky, and some of them can even be annoying. But they will all push you to explore these strange new worlds in ways you wouldn't have thought of!

ACHIEVEMENTS & TROPHIES!

Press to Boost

Achievement Purple Badger Don't Care

A Dyed Badger Ate Bees

COOLEST ACHIEVEMENT
ABZU

Achievement Breach
Leap from the water

Right at the start of the game, swim down into the depths of the ocean. Then hold the boost button and swim back toward the surface. You'll breach the water and shoot up into the air. Try it when you have fish following you to make the effect look even cooler.

CATCH THE BADGER
01 Just down from where you took the chivalry test you'll notice a shaking bush. Use the meat to catch the badger.

TURN BADGER PURPLE
02 Head into town and use the badger on the teeth-whitening liquid in the potion shop. This will turn the badger purple.

MOST ANNOYING TROPHY
JOURNEY

Trophy Reflection
Meditate with another player for 20 seconds

You meditate by leaving the controller alone. Don't press any buttons and you'll automatically go into a meditative state. The tricky part is getting another player to do this with you, as you can't communicate with them! Players are likely to try this near the start of the game but it will take luck to unlock this one.

FIND THE HONEY
03 In the picnic area past where you found the meat, shake the tree so the beehive falls down. Use the badger on the beehive.

ACHIEVEMENTS & TROPHIES!

QUICKEST ACHIEVEMENT

GRIM FANDANGO

🏆 **Achievement** "What I did back in the fat days is none of your business"

Ask Eva how she got stuck here

Find your secretary, Eva. Talk to her until the option comes up to ask her how she got stuck there. When she gives her reply, that'll be the challenge completed. This should take you less than a minute to unlock.

It's my boss' secretary, Eva.

WEIRDEST TROPHY

SONG OF THE DEEP

🏆 **Trophy** The Inner Sanctum

Commune with the giant seahorse

It's not every day you have a conversation with a giant seahorse but you do in *Song of the Deep*. Collect the three parts of the destroyed clockwork seahorse, then repair the broken seahorse in Seagarden. A new path opens up and you'll get to have a conversation with a giant seahorse.

FUNNIEST TROPHY

BACK TO THE FUTURE

🏆 **Trophy** Moonwalker

Bust a move, 80s style

In the final episode, you'll find yourself at an Expo with an "Experience the wonder of the continuuophone" Theremin booth. To unlock this you will need to keep interacting with the stand and eventually, Marty McFly will bust out the most iconic of all 80s dance moves—the Moonwalk.

MOST AWESOME TROPHY

ORI AND THE BLIND FOREST

🏆 **Trophy** Deadly Detonation
Kill 4 enemies simultaneously using Charge Flame

A fantastic achievement because of the explosive fireworks caused by the Charge Flame attack! The large pink blob enemies explode into smaller blobs when they're first attacked. Just hit this group of smaller enemies with the Charge Flame to complete the challenge.

EASIEST ACHIEVEMENTS

BEYOND EYES

🏆 **Achievement** Courage
When you find the cow, take the nearby flower and feed it. The first time you'll get scared, so feed it again, unlocking the Courage achievement or trophy.

ANOTHER WORLD: 20TH ANNIVERSARY EDITION

🏆 **Achievement** Survivor
Run to the right and when the beast attacks, run left. Grab the vine and when it breaks, run to the right again.

THE SECRET OF MONKEY ISLAND: REMASTERED

🏆 **Achievement** Ten Minutes Later
Can Guybrush Threepwood hold his breath underwater for 10 minutes? Of course not. However, you'll get an achievement for trying, so just leave the pad alone for 10 minutes.

END GAME

....

JOURNEY
Forever friend

This *Game On* adventure is over ... but that doesn't mean your story should stop just yet! Wait at the beginning of *Journey* for another player to show up and you can play through the entire adventure together, from start to finish. It's a magical experience.